Orchids on Glass

an Adult Coloring Book

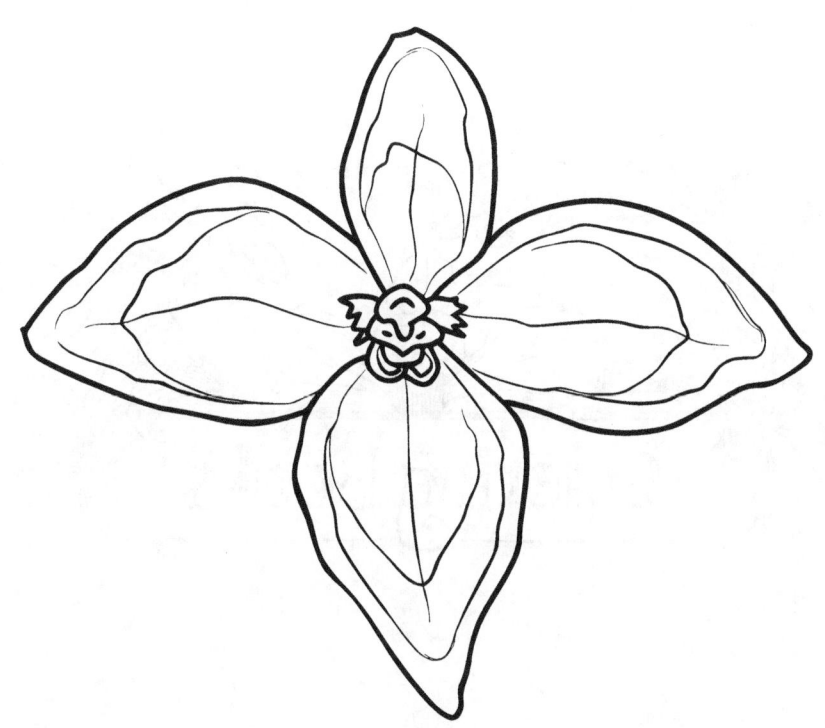

by Tes Scholtz

Artwork Anywhere™

Color this!
Yours could be our new facebook cover photo!
Get more info and download printable copies at
ArtworkAnywhere.com/fb

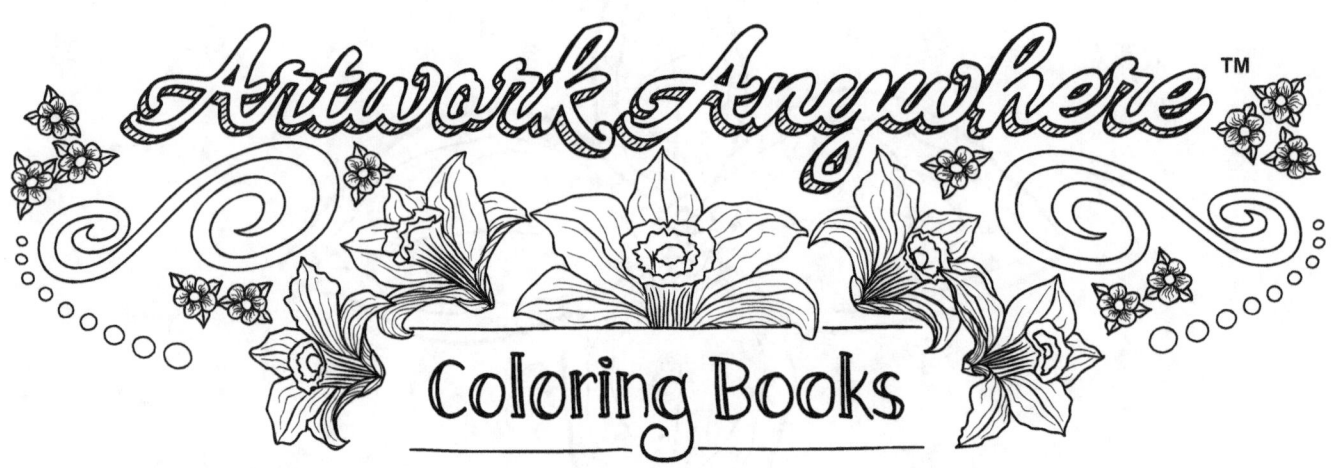

Artwork Anywhere™
Coloring Books

Cover: The front and back cover were designed and colored by Tes Scholtz.
Hand coloring was done with Derwent ® Inktense pencils.

Orchids on Glass
an Adult Coloring Book

by Tes Scholtz

Artwork Anywhere ™

Orchids on Glass adult coloring book features 25 hand drawn illustrations depicting a variety of lush orchids on simple yet dynamic backgrounds inspired by the beautiful look of colorful stained glass windows. Some are intricate and complex, others are simpler and flowing, to suit your many coloring moods. "*Les Orchidées: Histoire Iconographique*", 1880, which is in the public domain, was used for reference.

"I hope you enjoy coloring it as much as I enjoyed drawing it, which is a lot!!" ~Tes

Use colored pencils, crayons, inks, gel pens, markers, whatever you want, or mix it up and use them all! There are no rules. There are suggestions, though: Some markers and paints may bleed through the pages. To avoid damaging other pages, use a barrier sheet between pages, or remove the page from the book before coloring.

 ArtworkAnywhere.com

Be sure to check out ArtworkAnywhere.com for our latest coloring books, plus updates, contests, and exclusive free coloring pages!

We love to see your work! Please share your favorite colorings, so we can show it off! Please visit ArtworkAnywhere.com/social to see where we are on social media @artworkanywhere!

Do you have questions, criticism, compliments, ideas? Send your thoughts to: suggestions@artworkanywhere.com

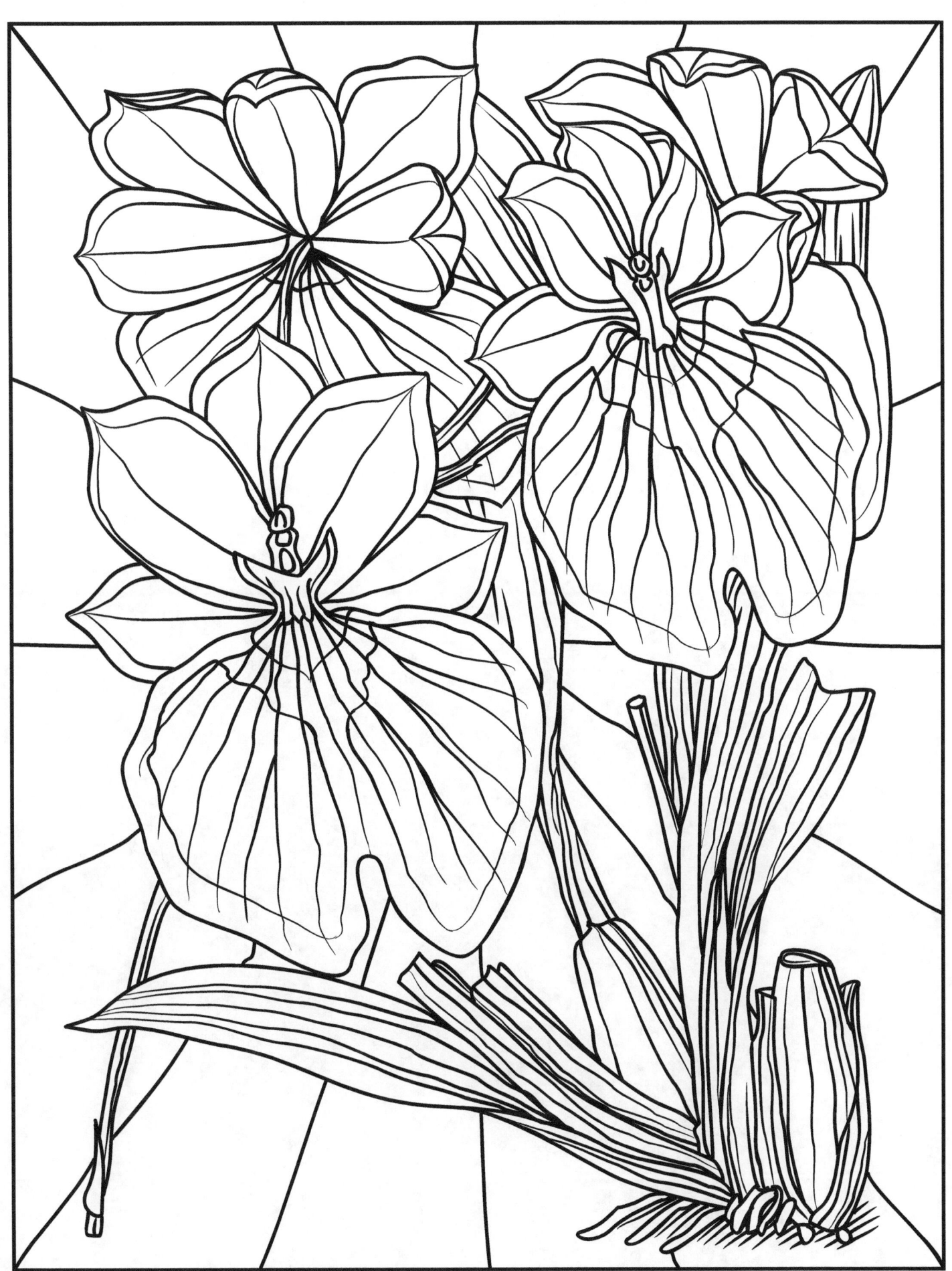

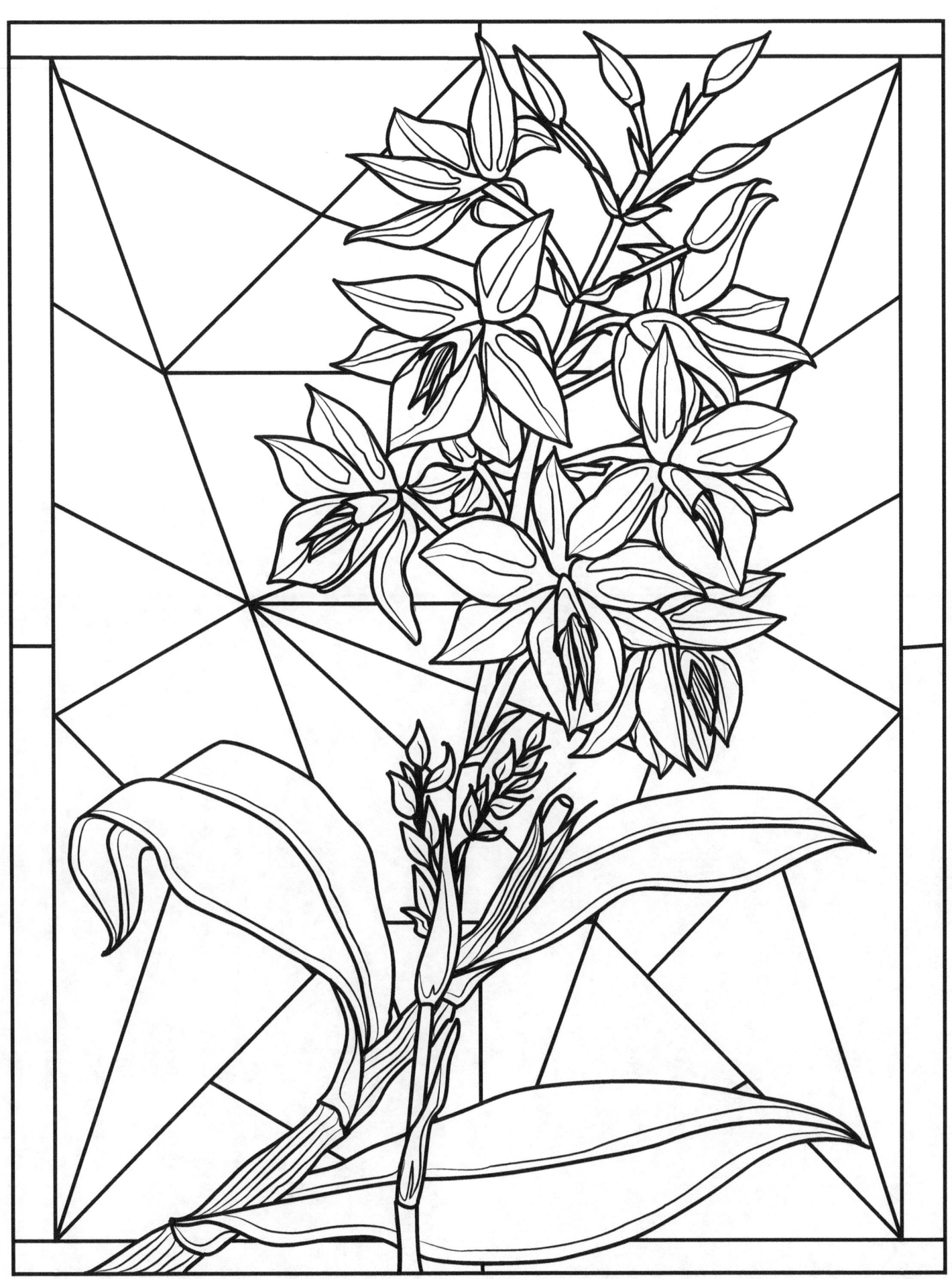

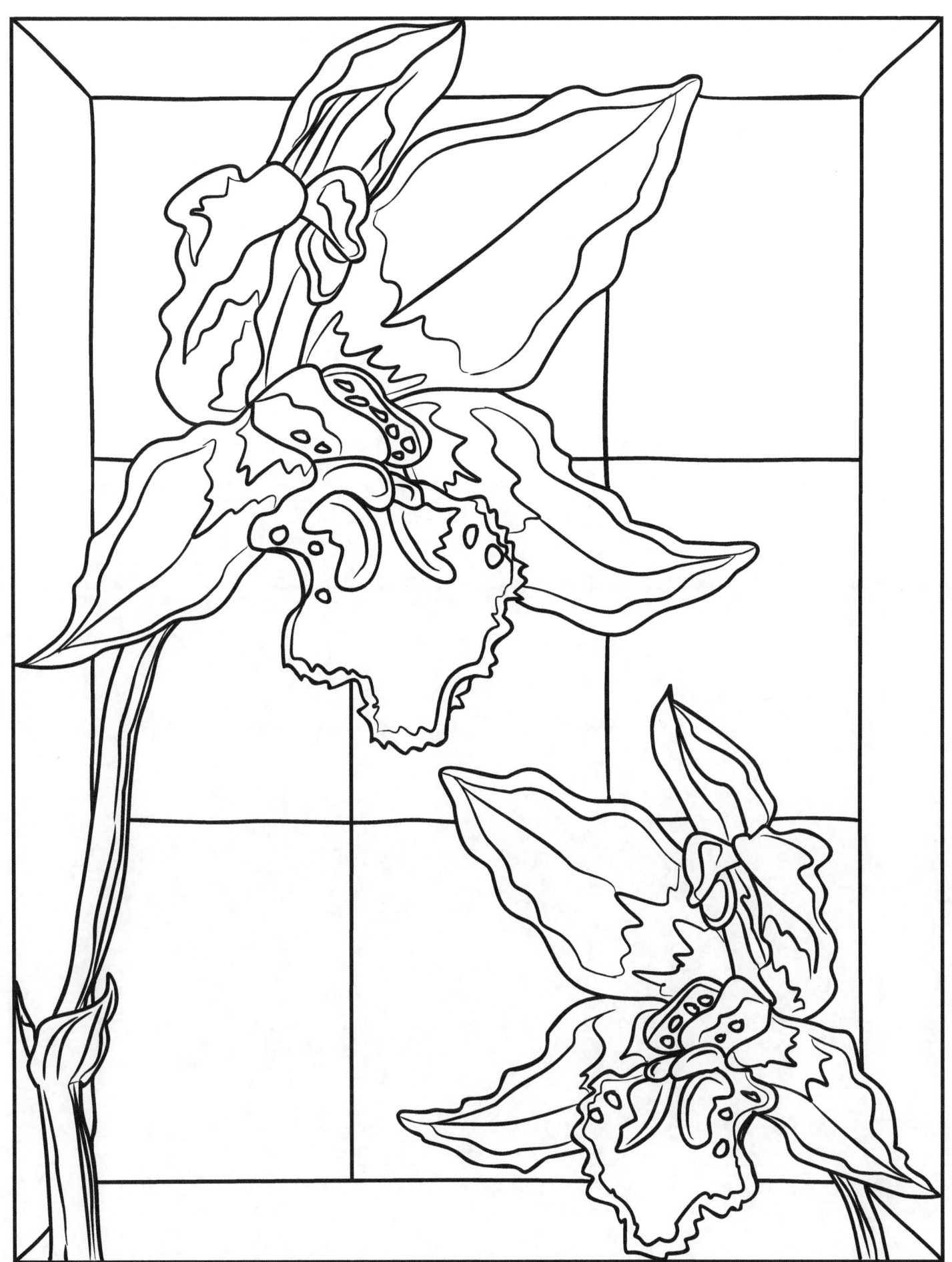

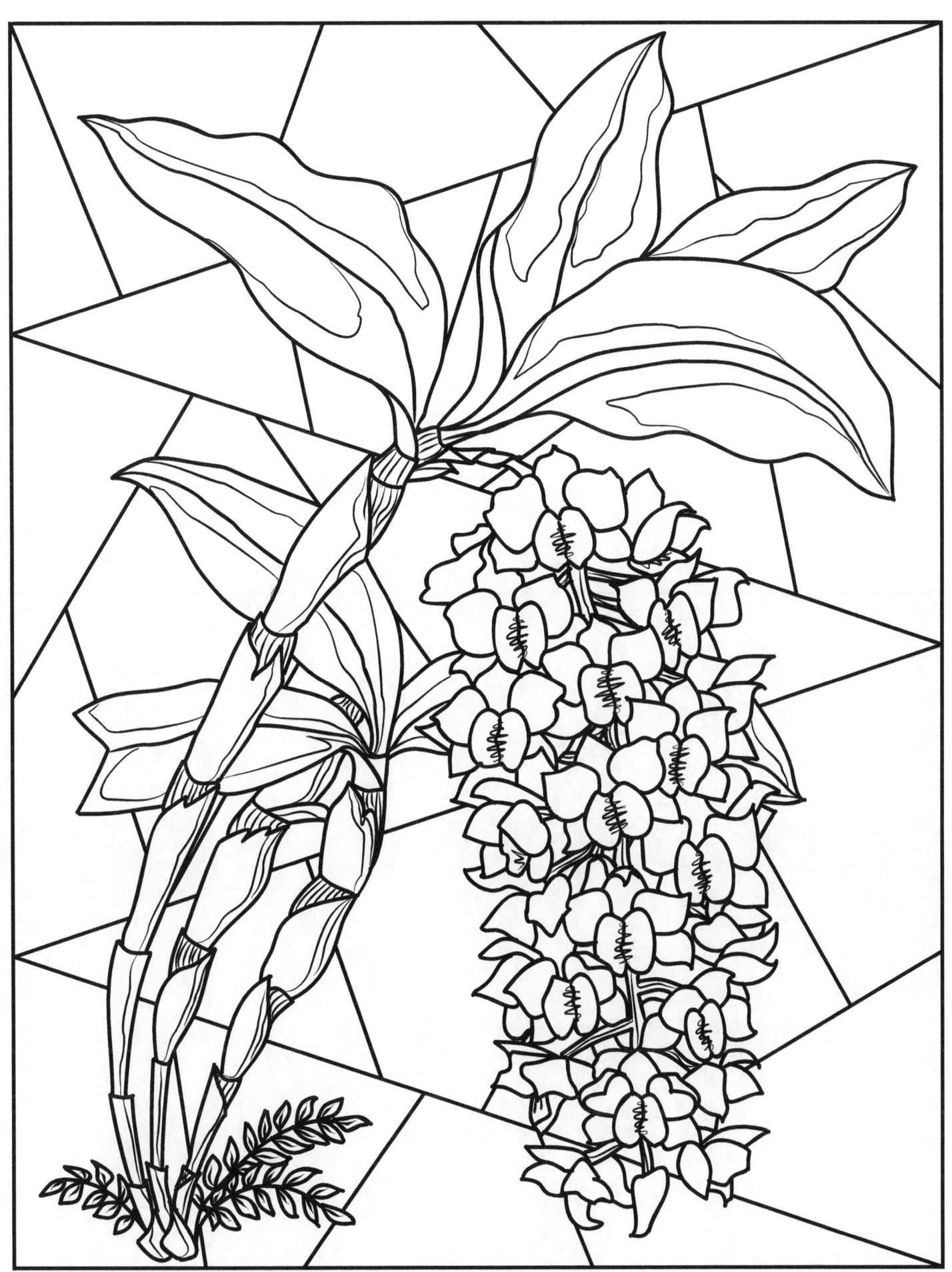

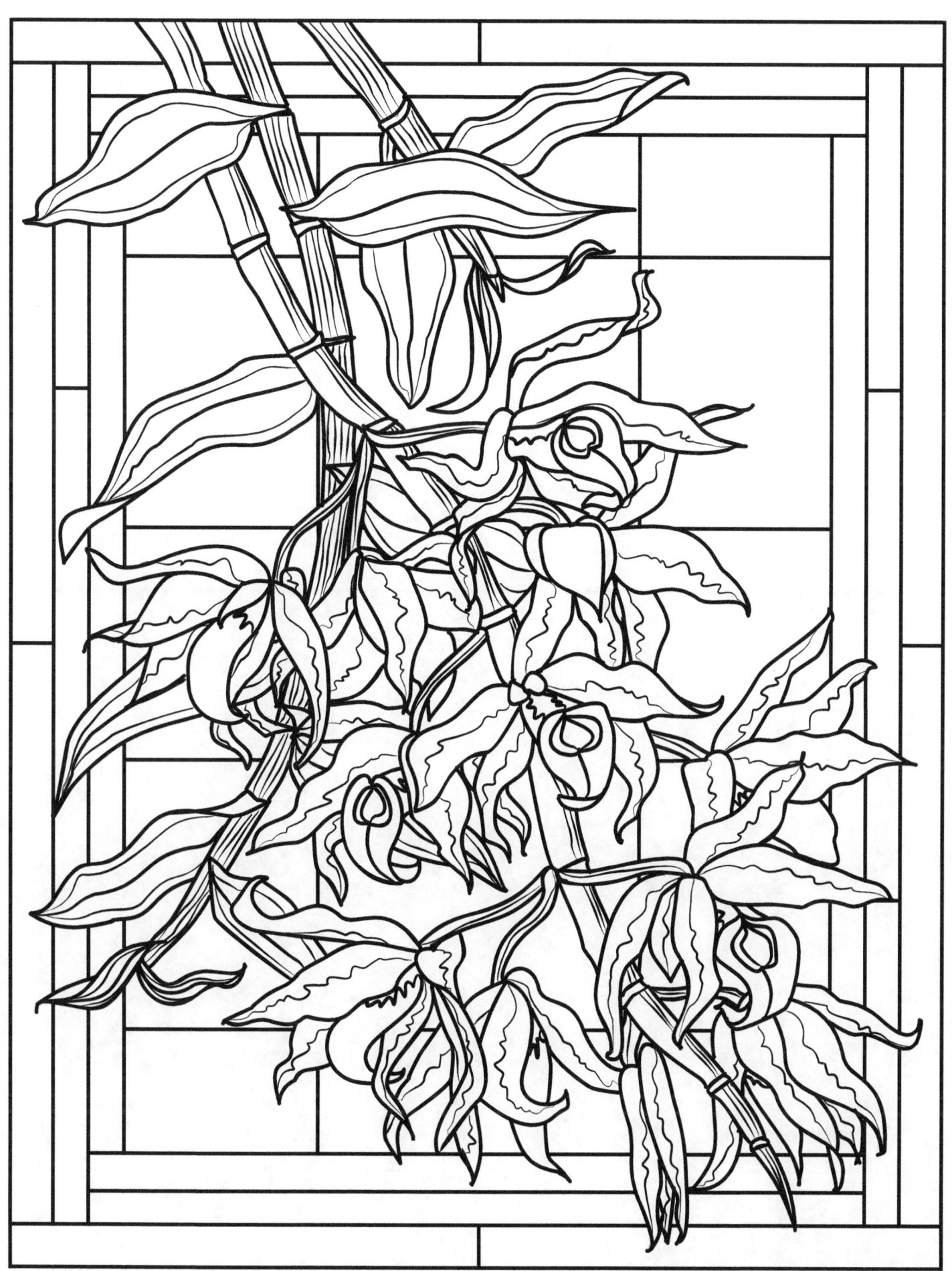

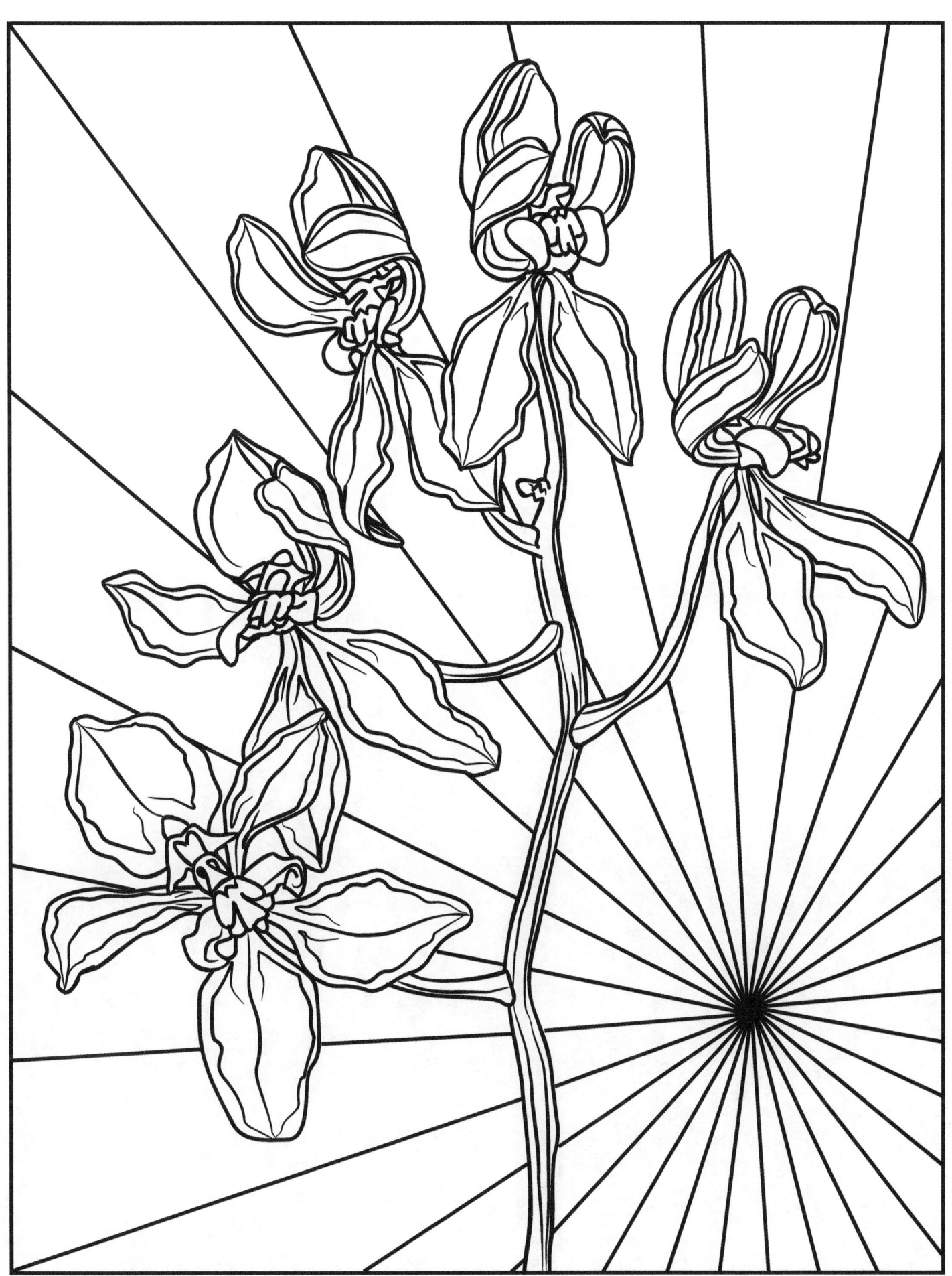

ArtworkAnywhere.com

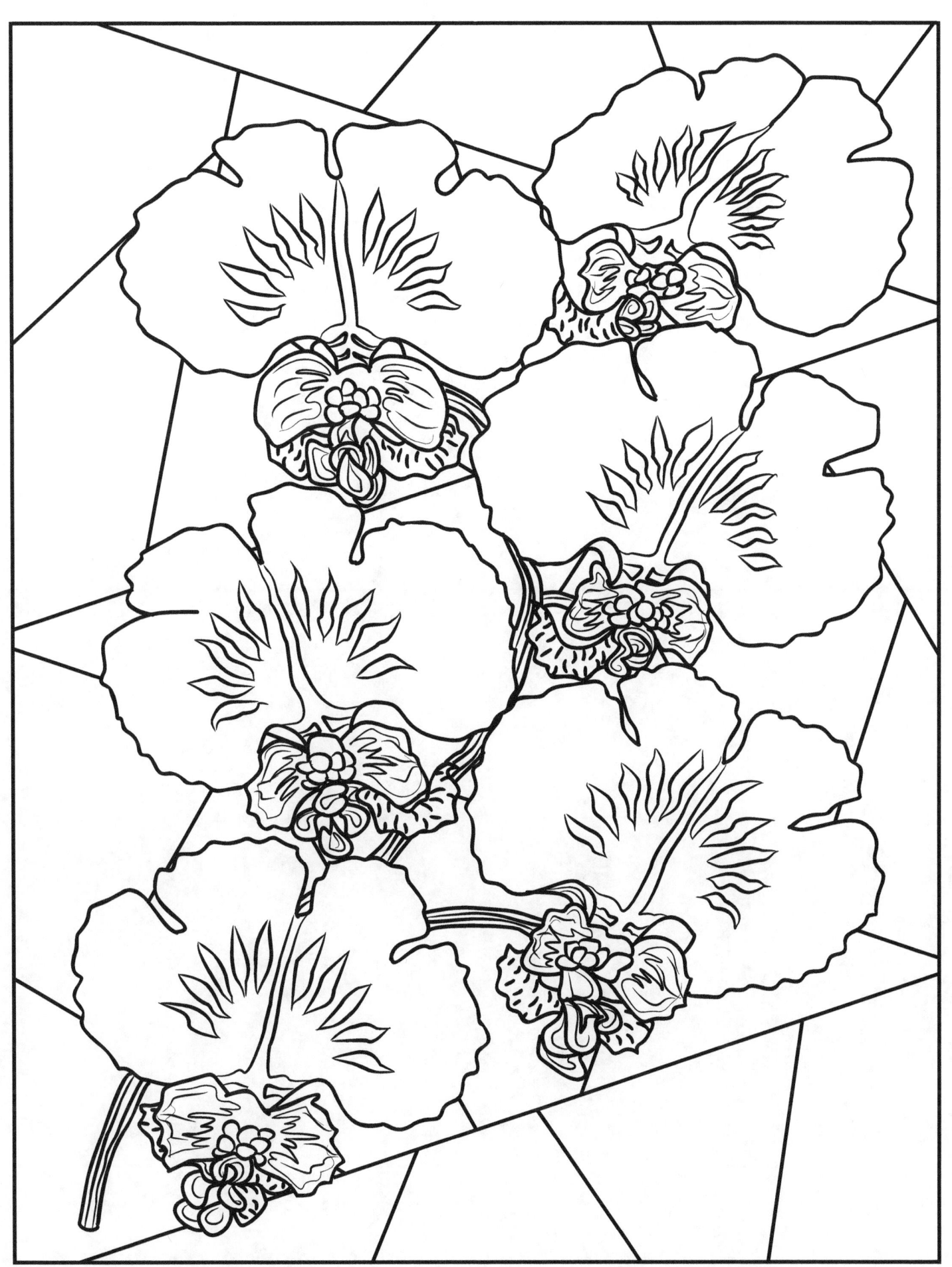

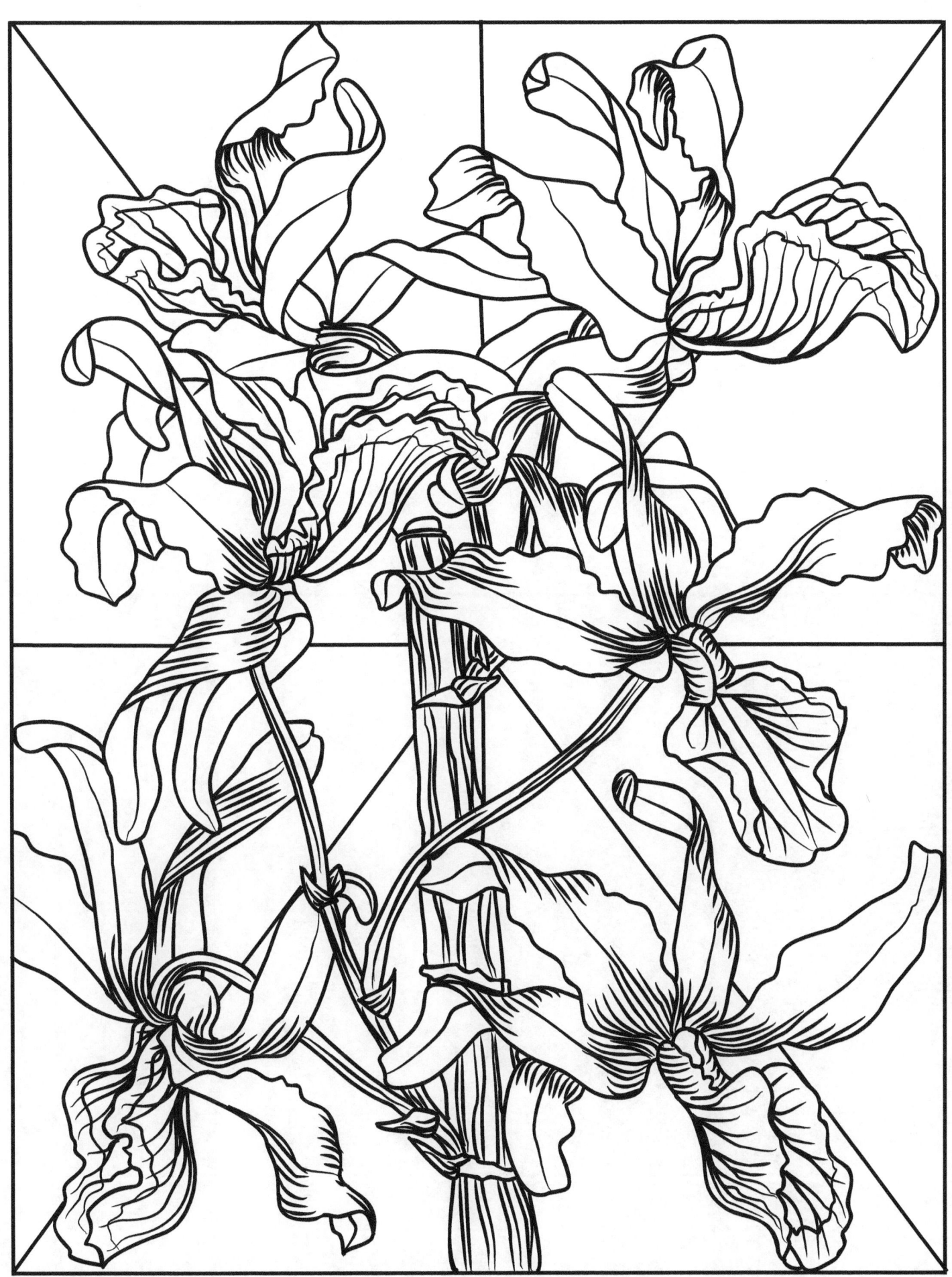

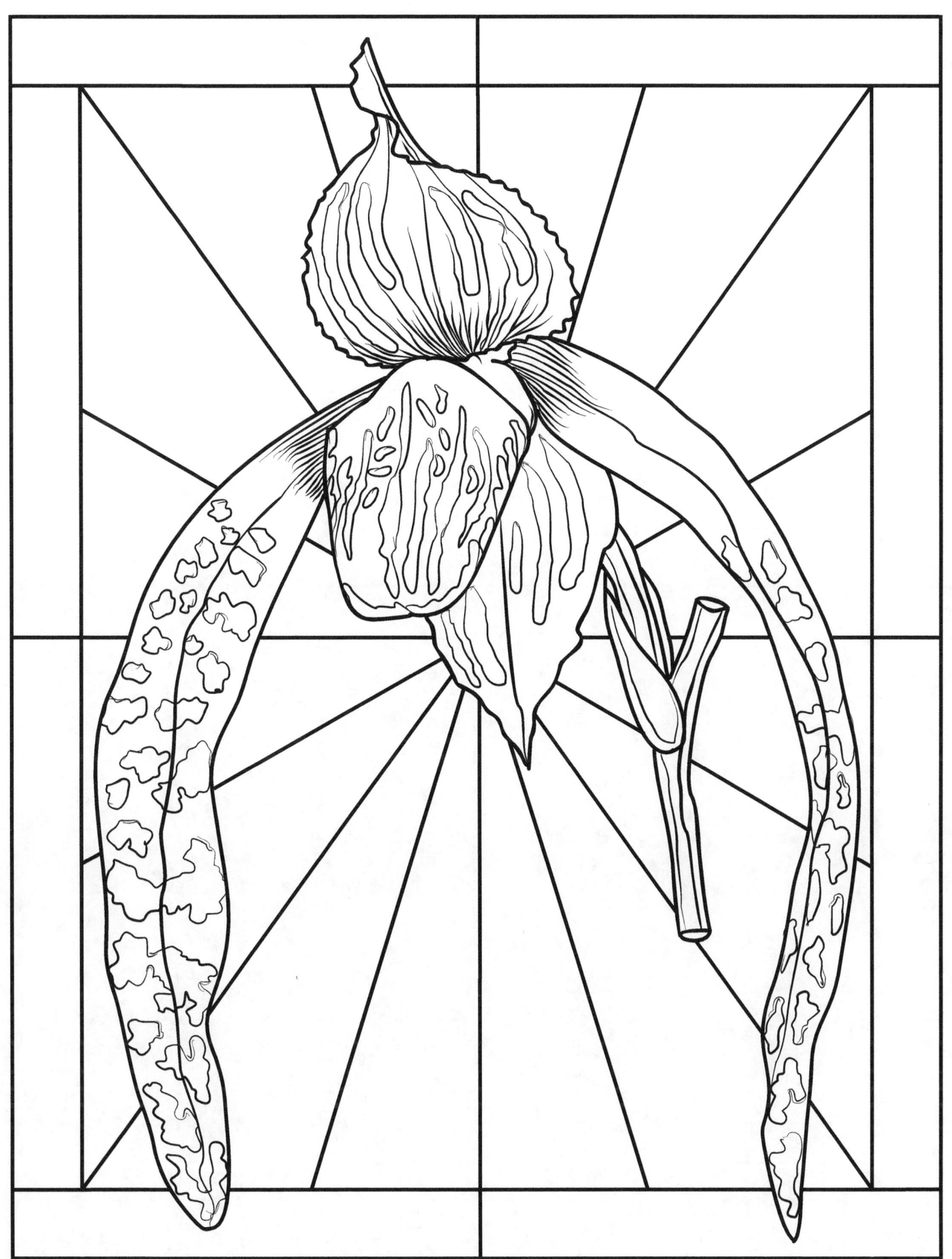

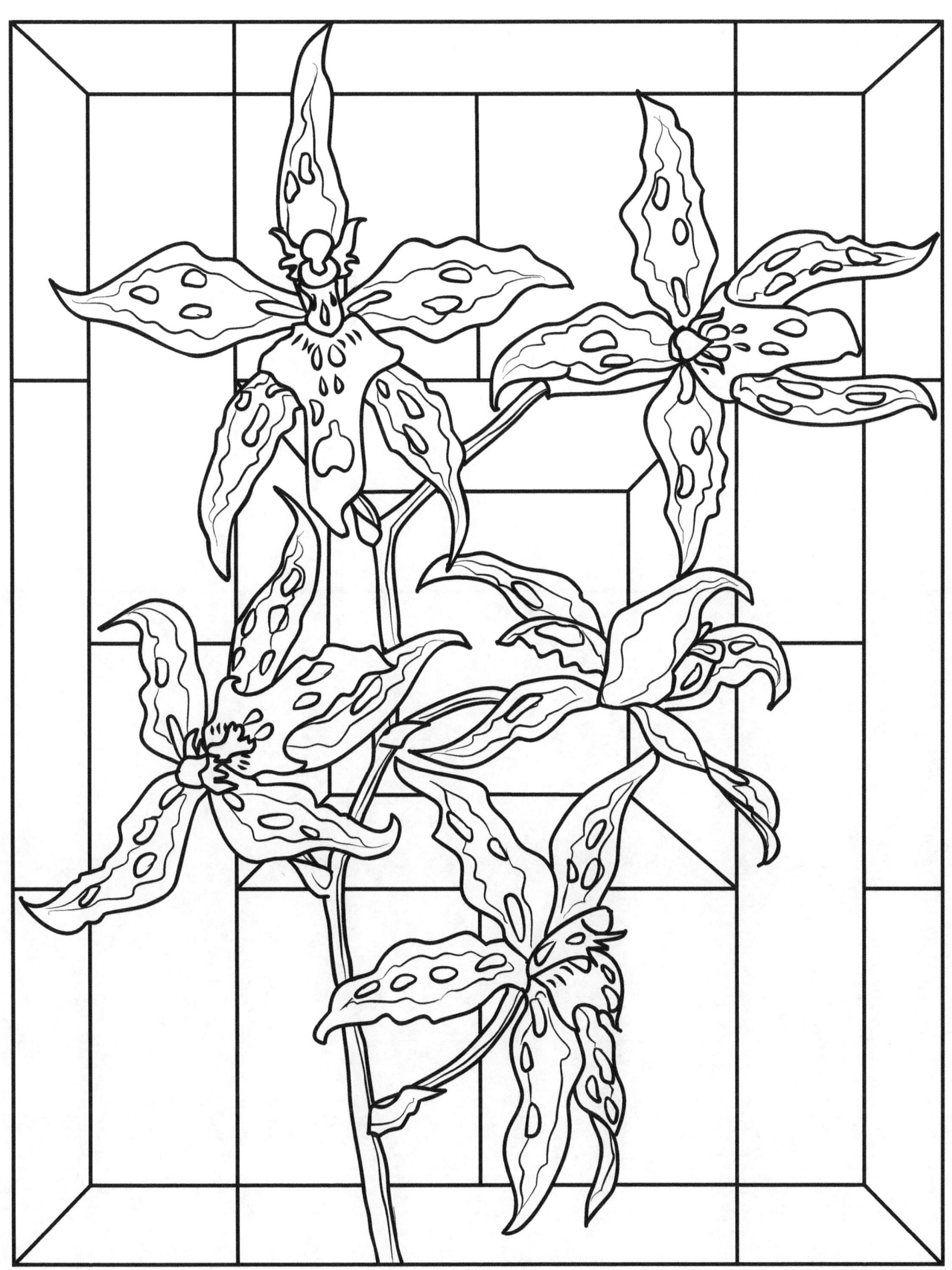

ArtworkAnywhere.com

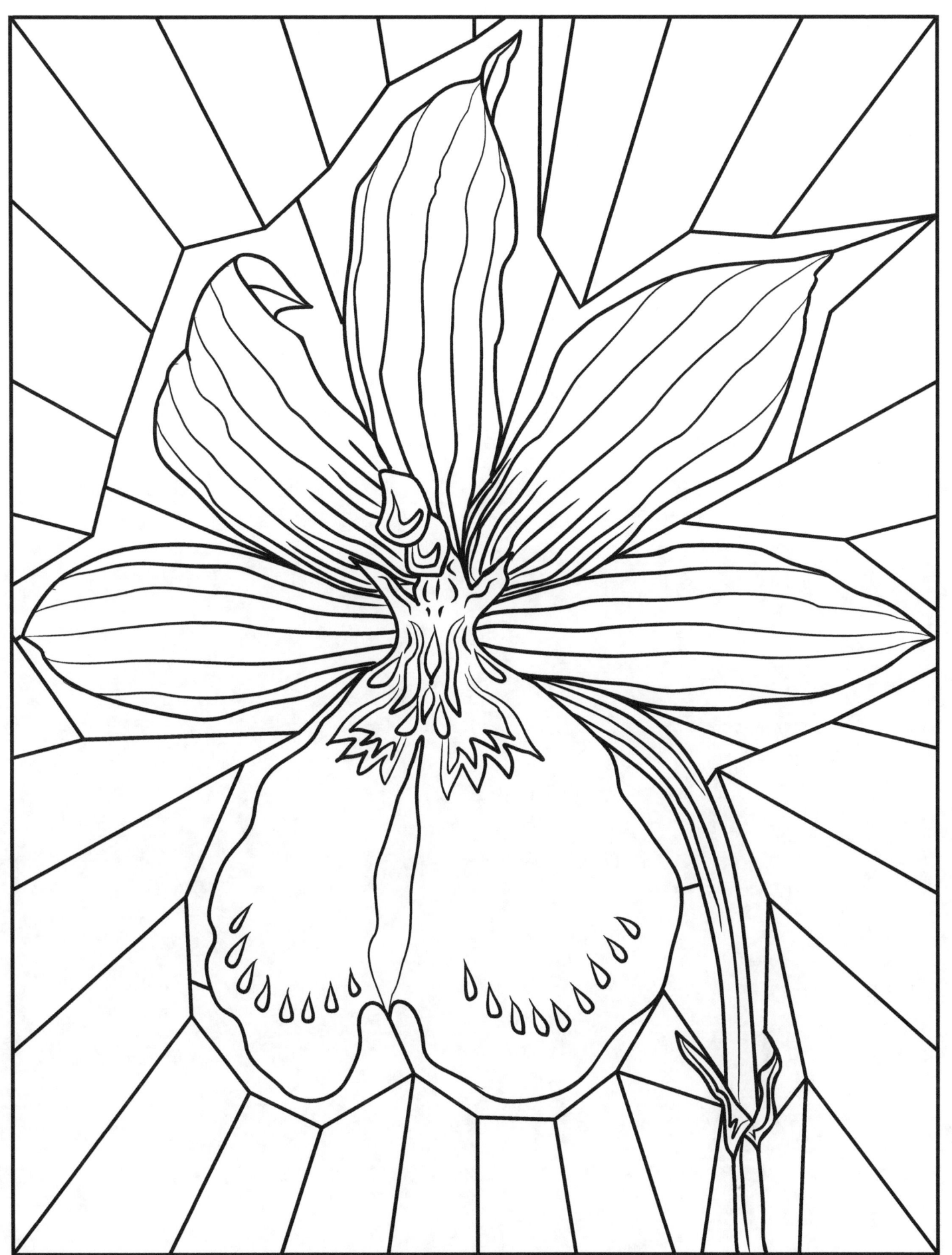

ArtworkAnywhere.com

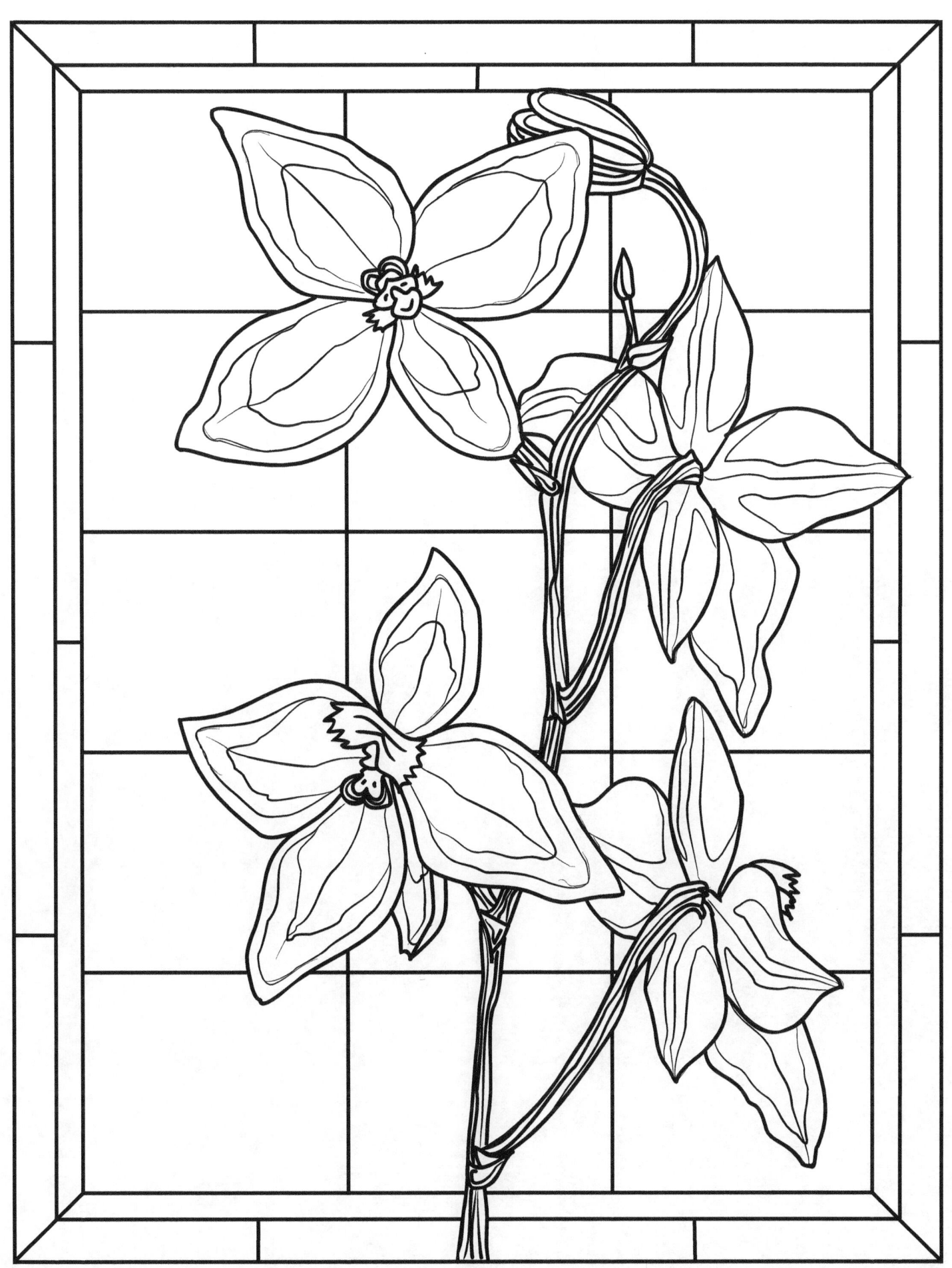

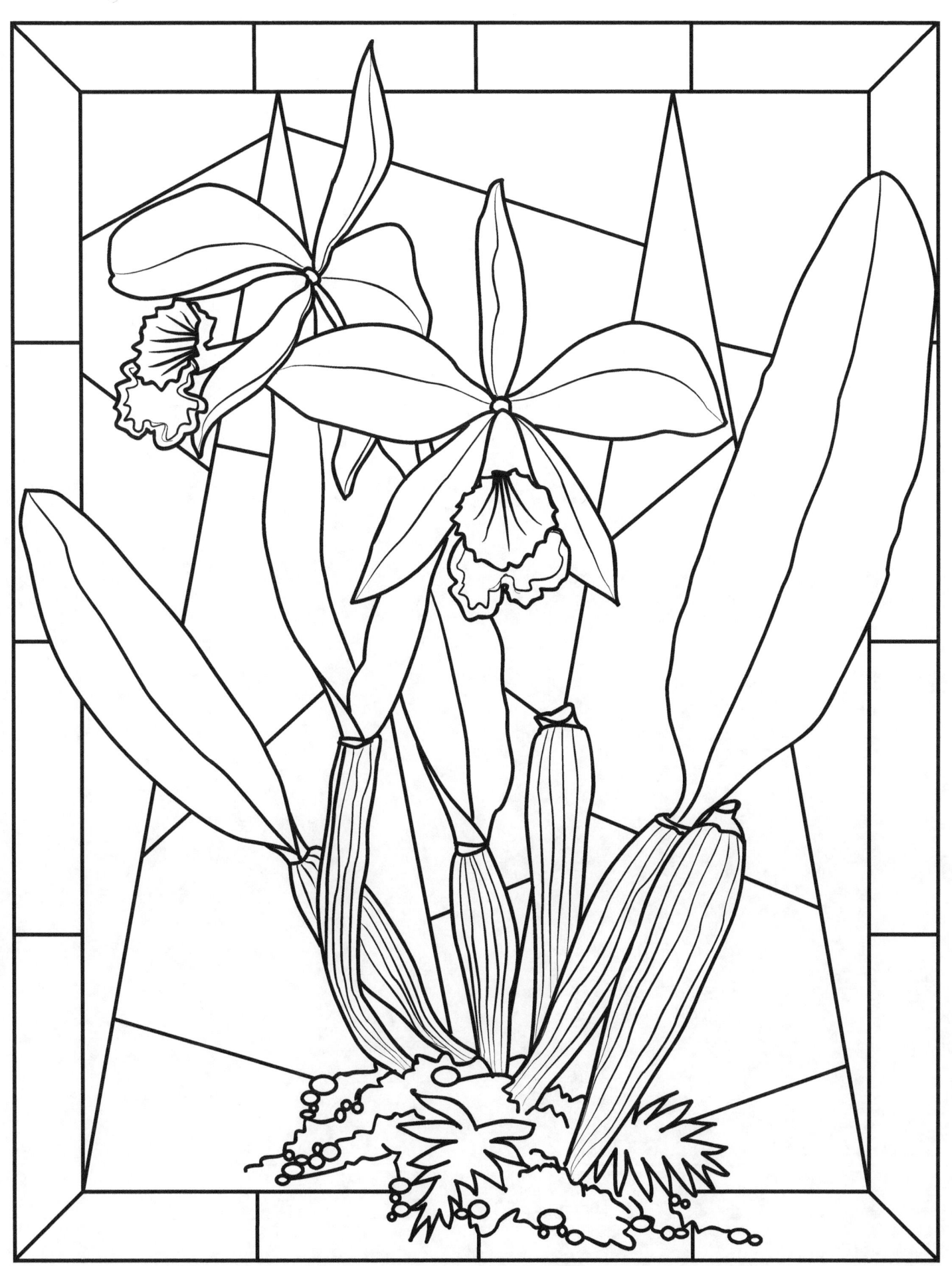

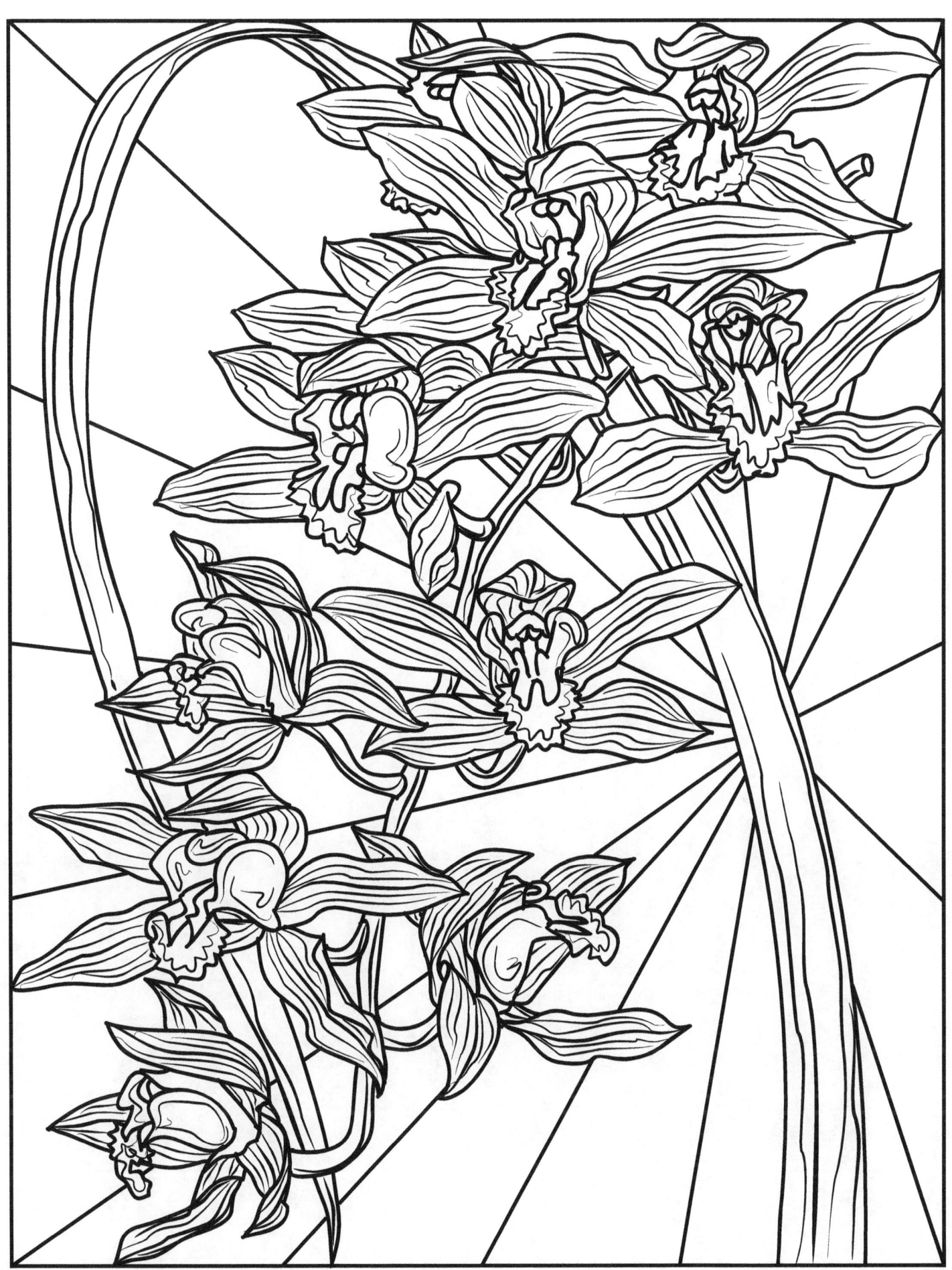

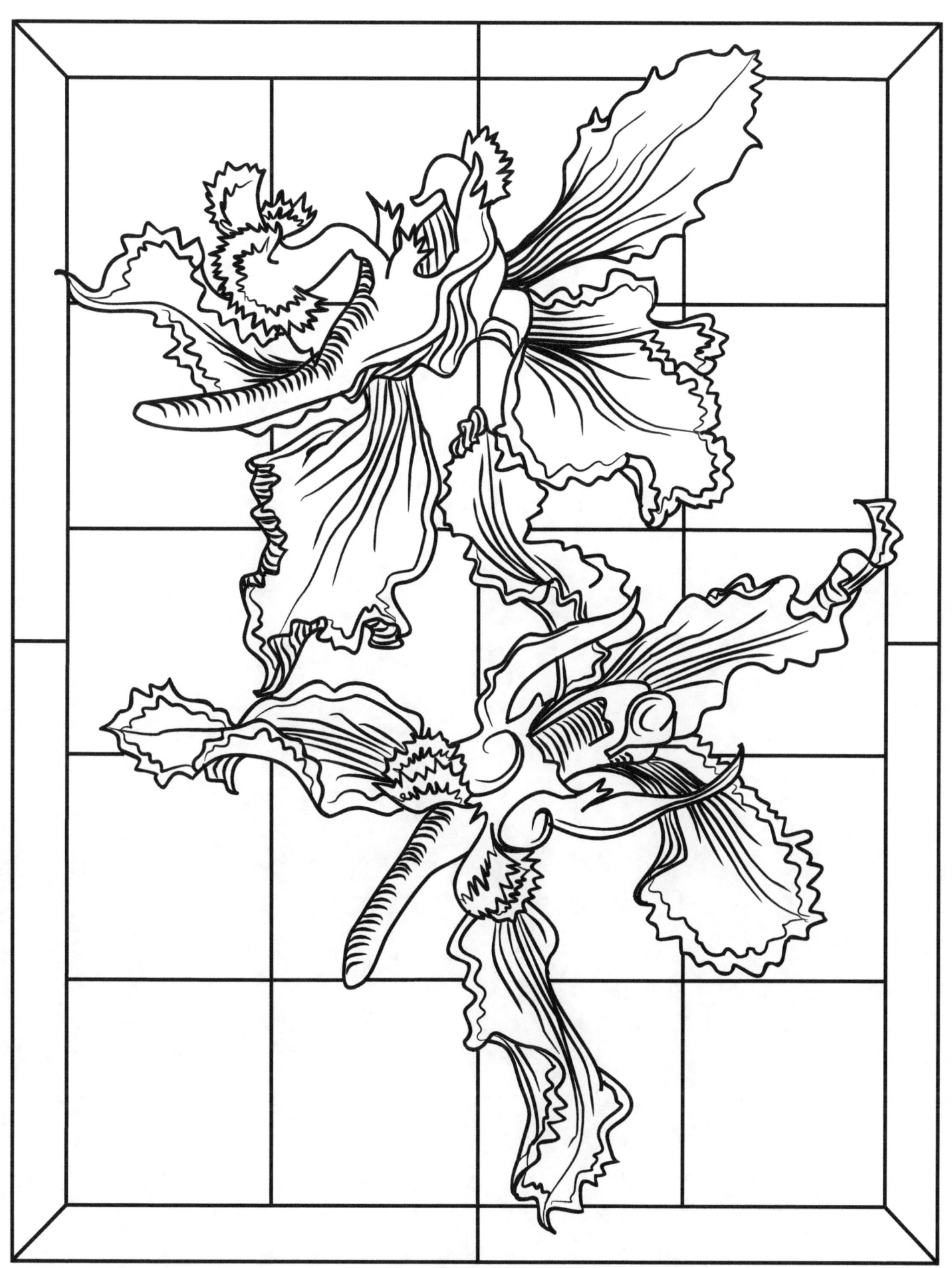

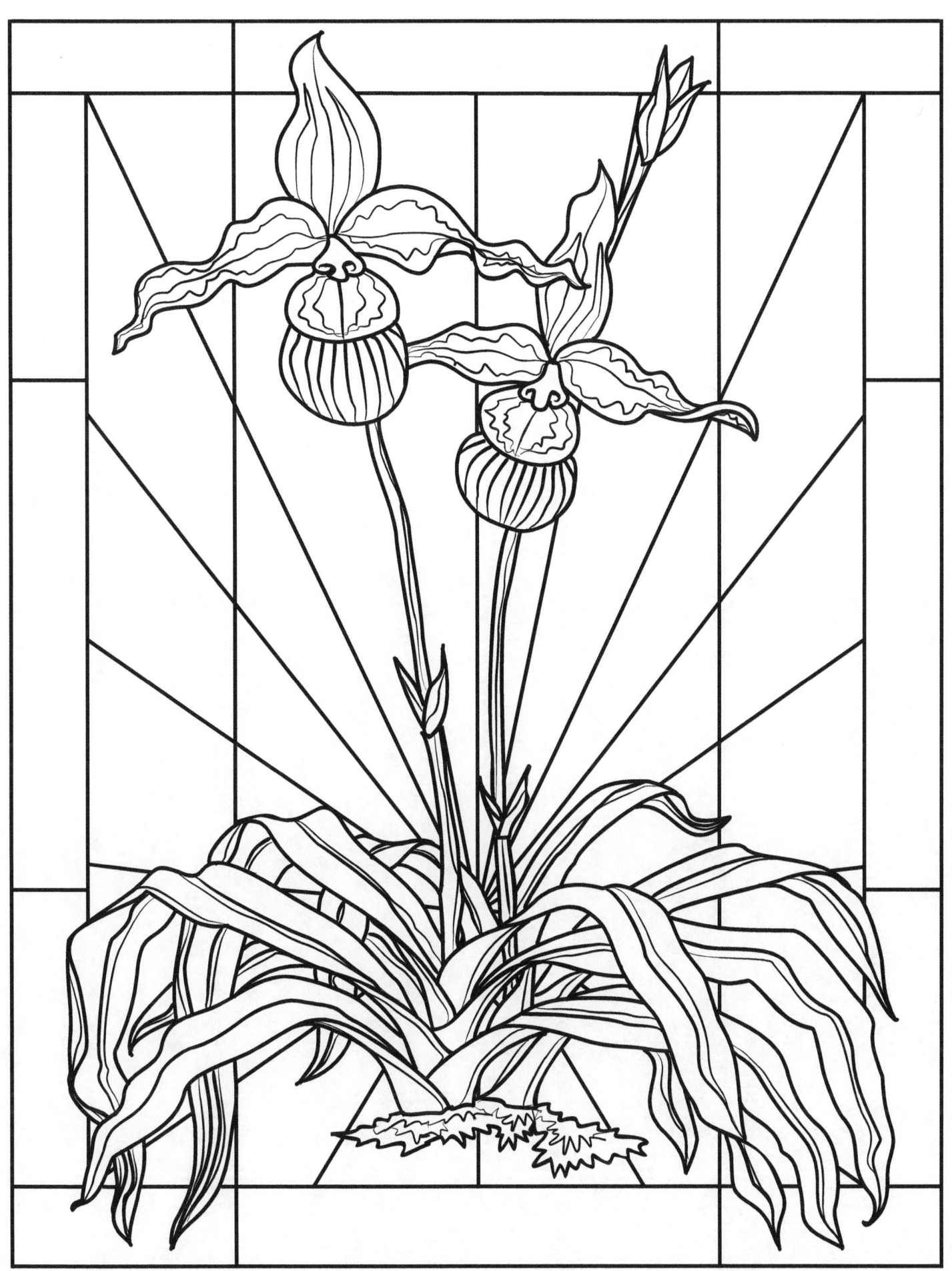

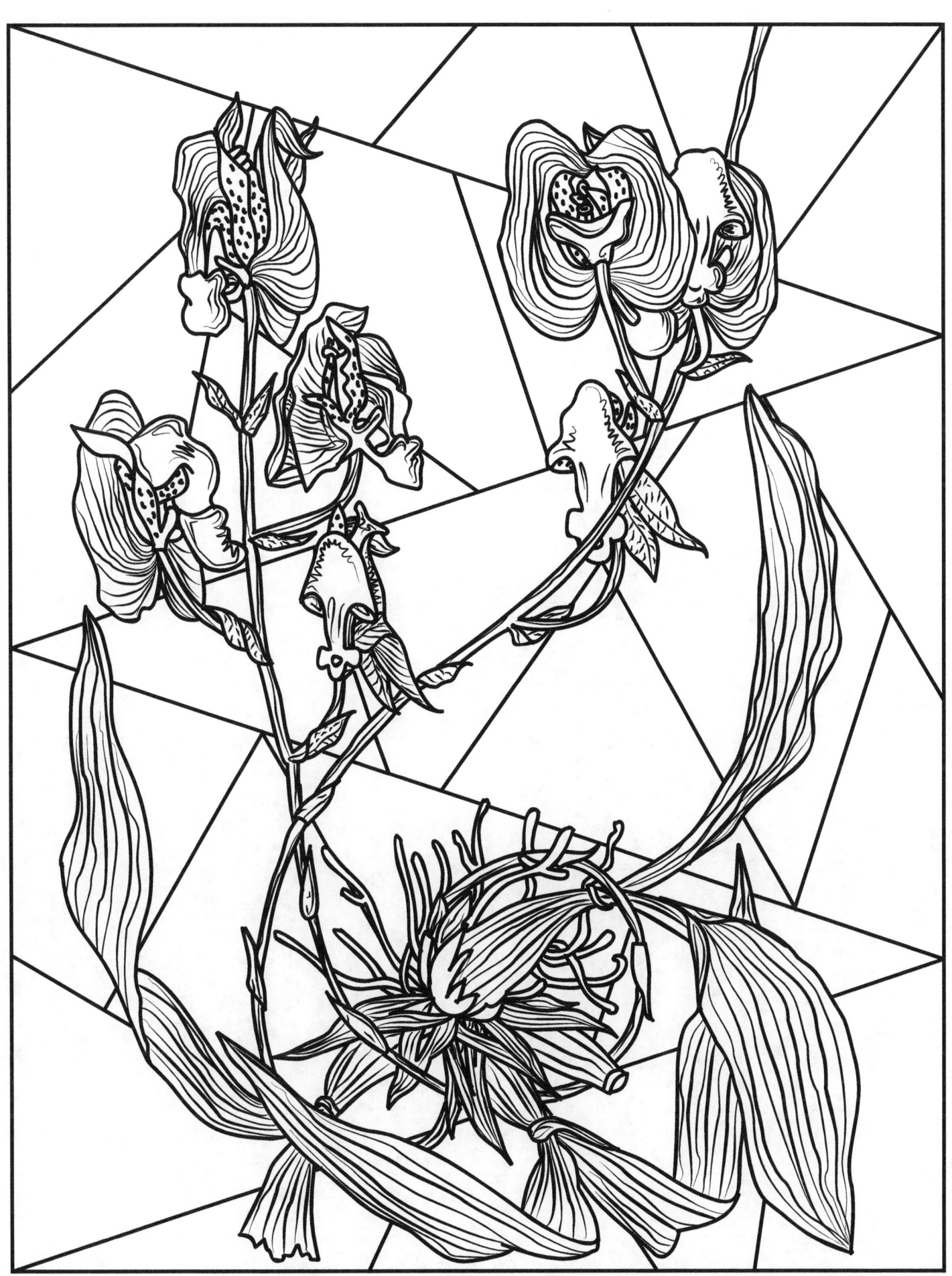

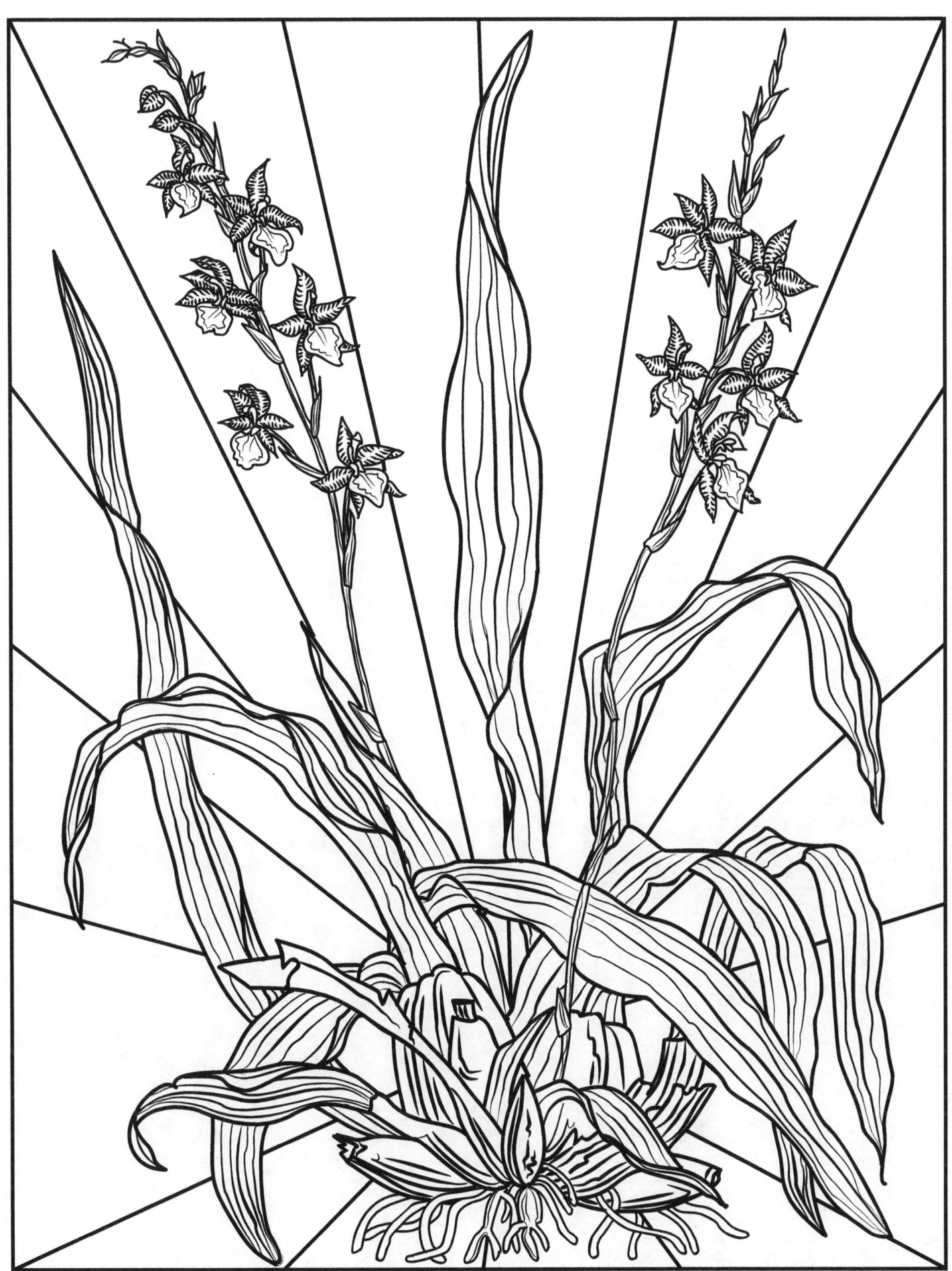

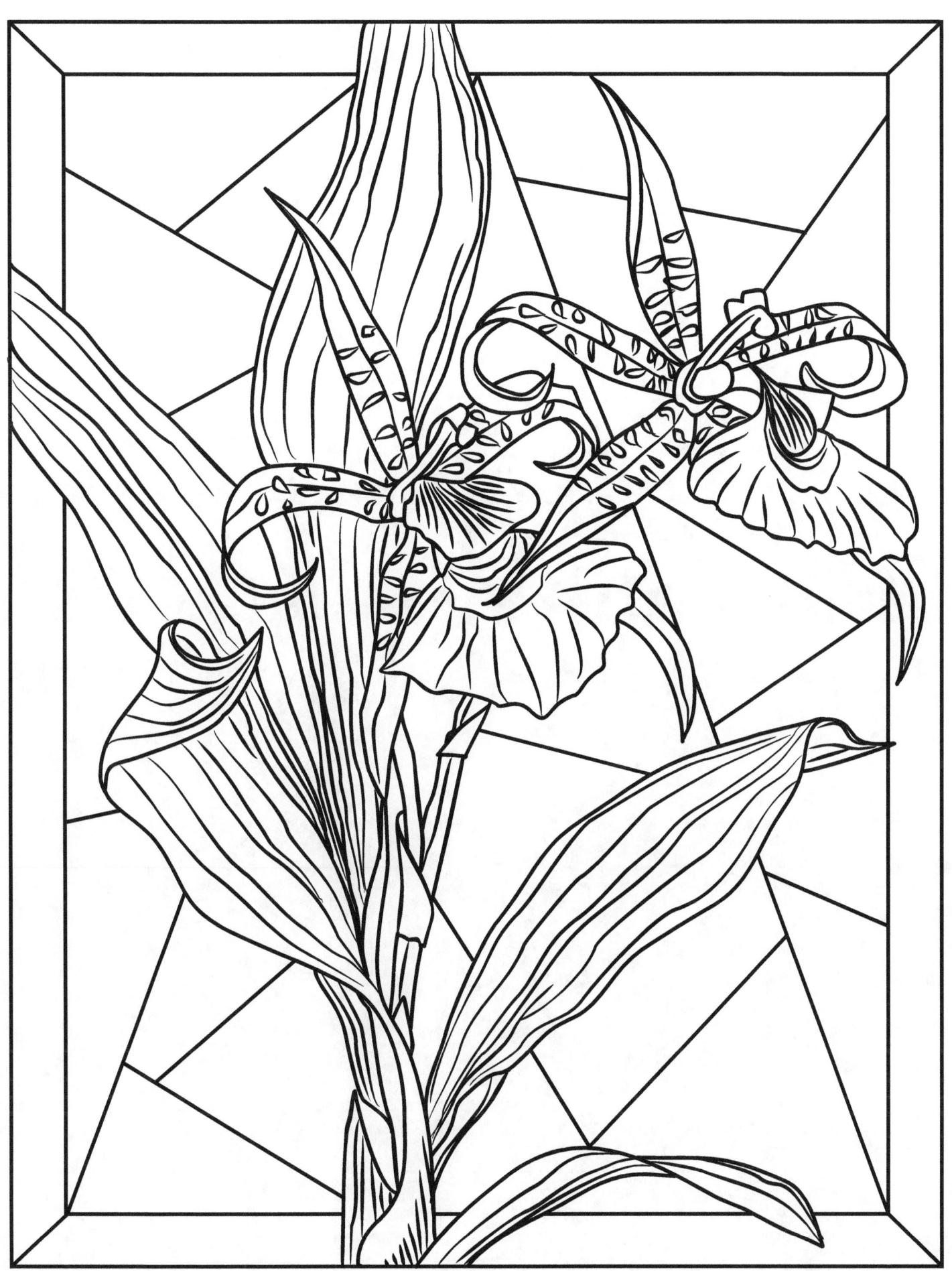

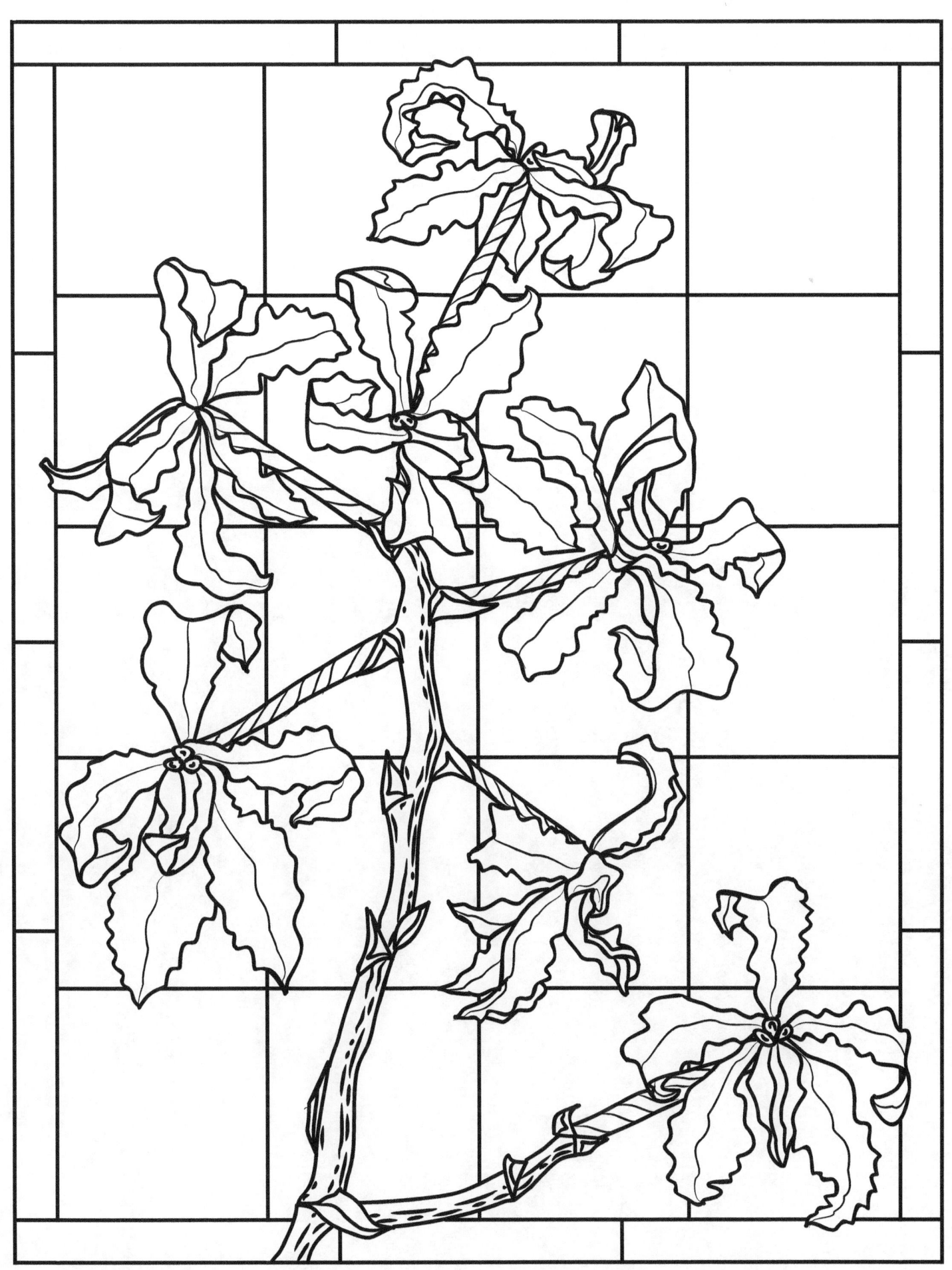

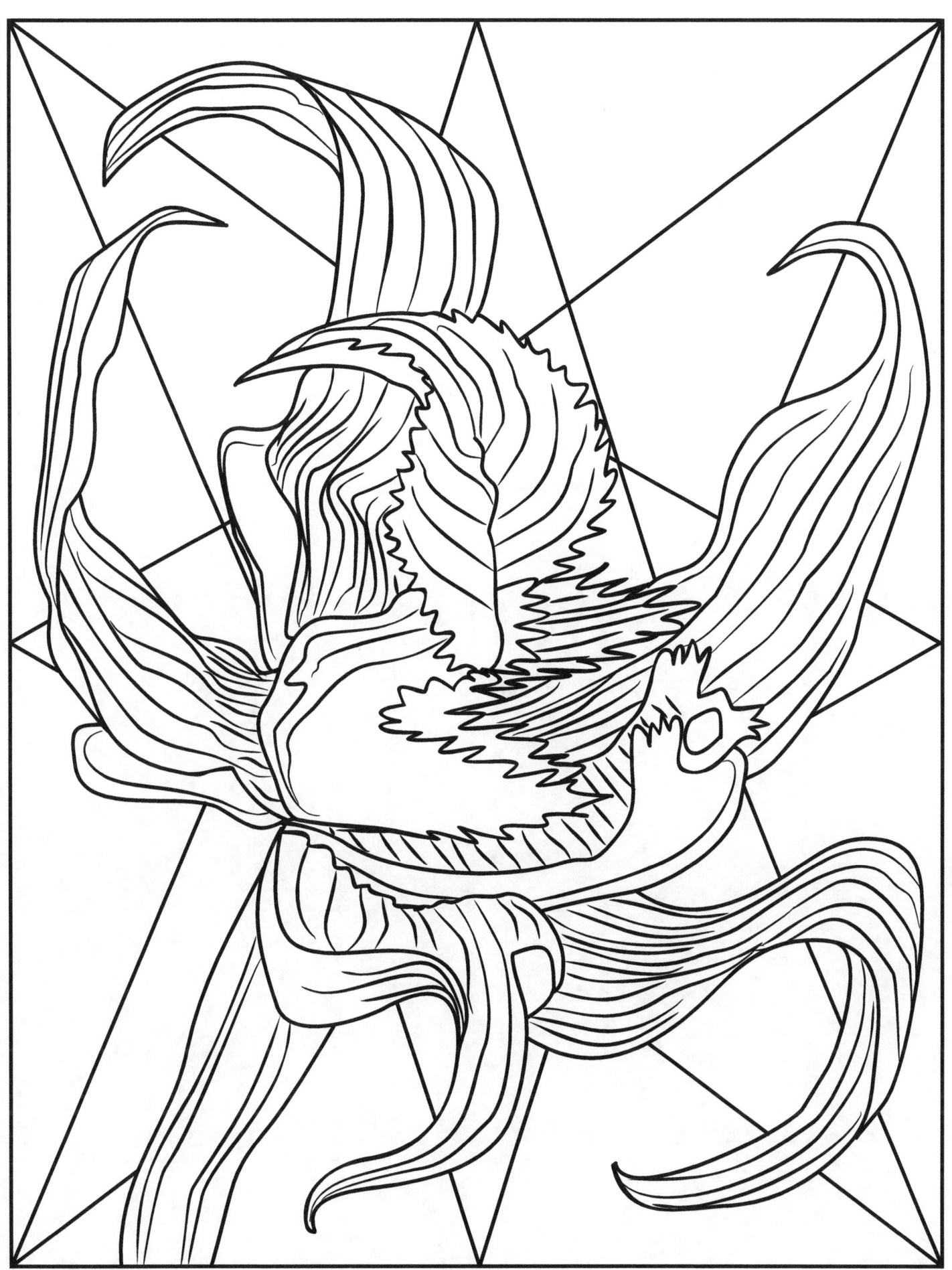

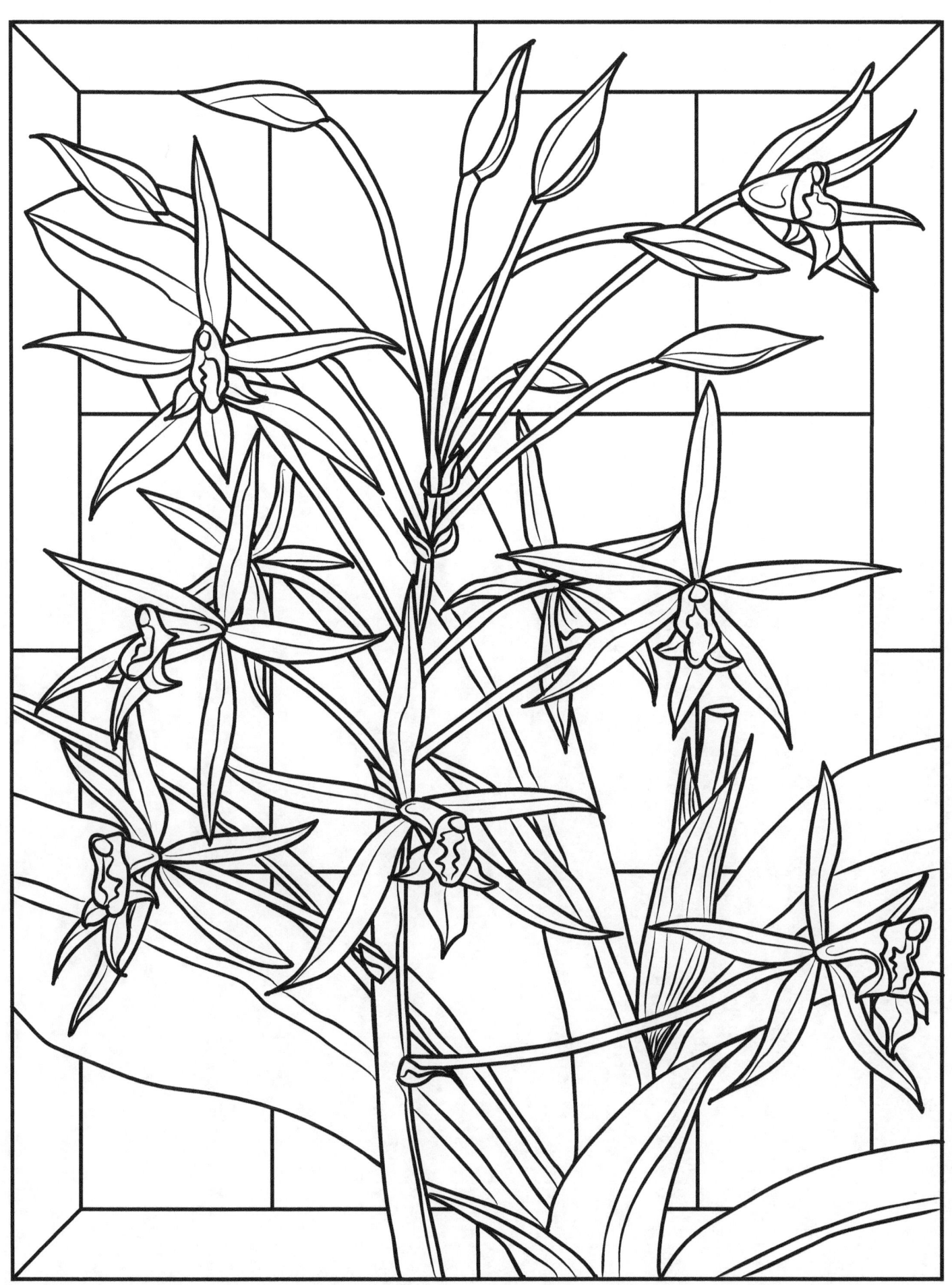

ArtworkAnywhere.com

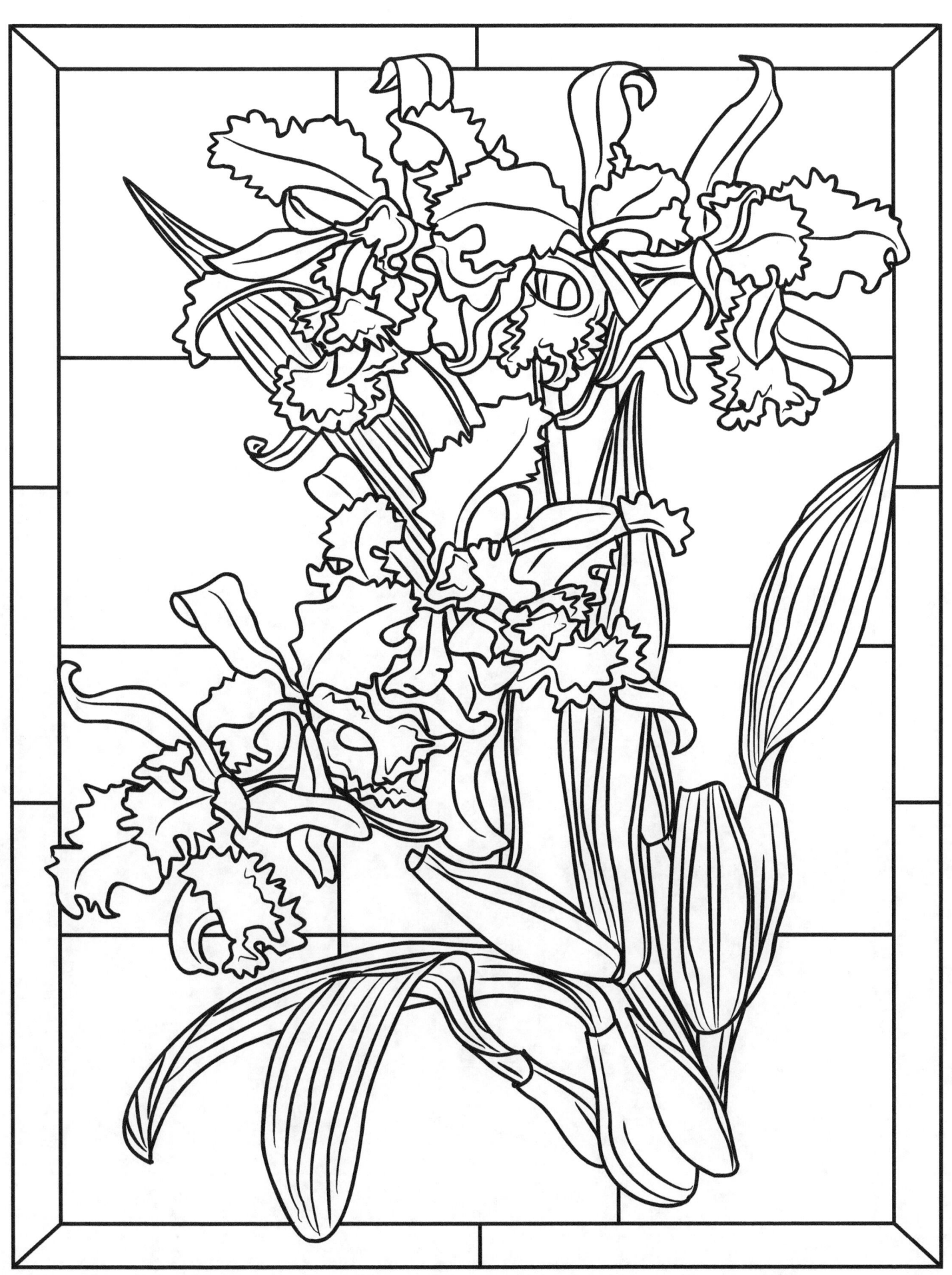

ArtworkAnywhere.com

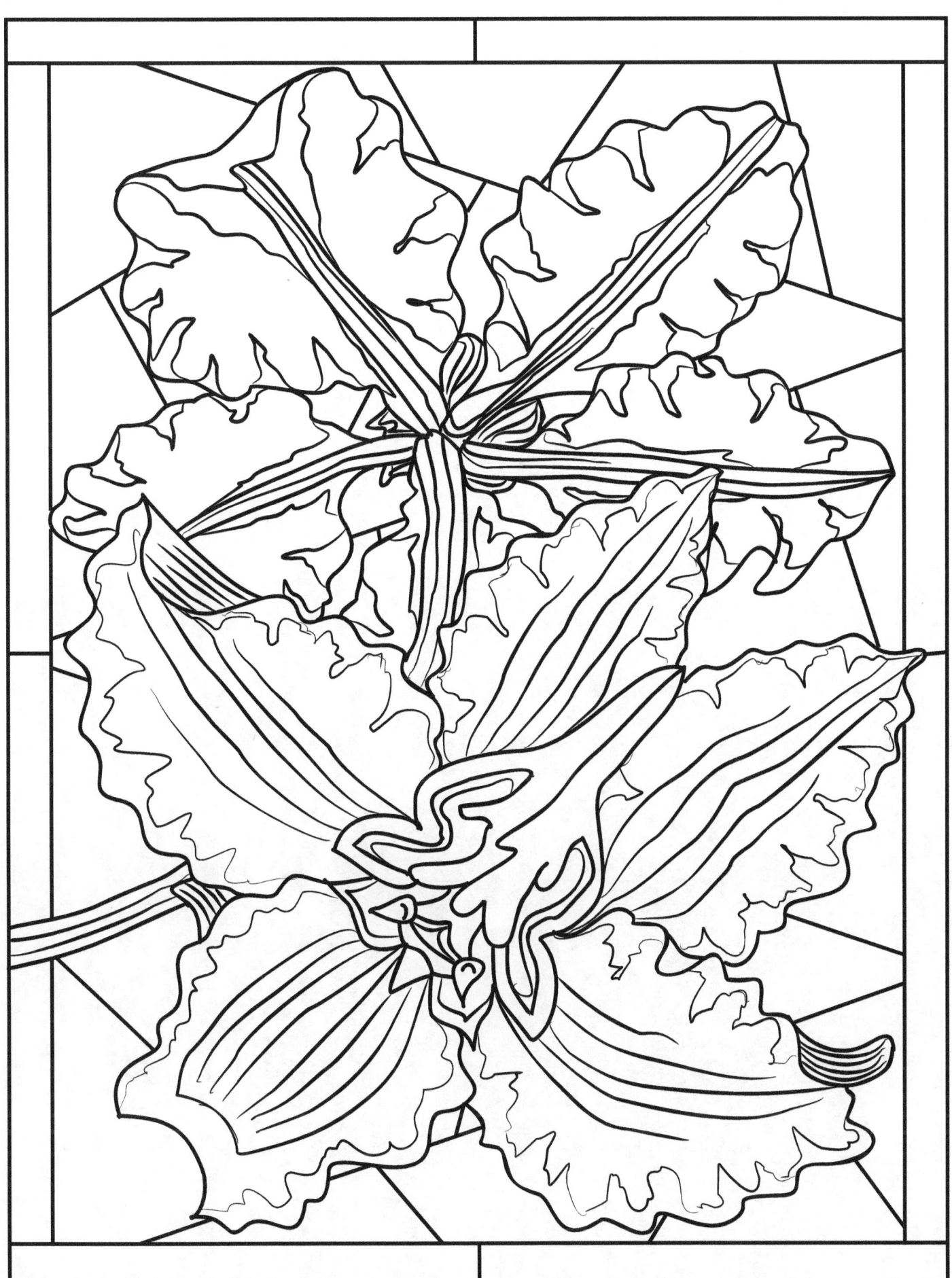

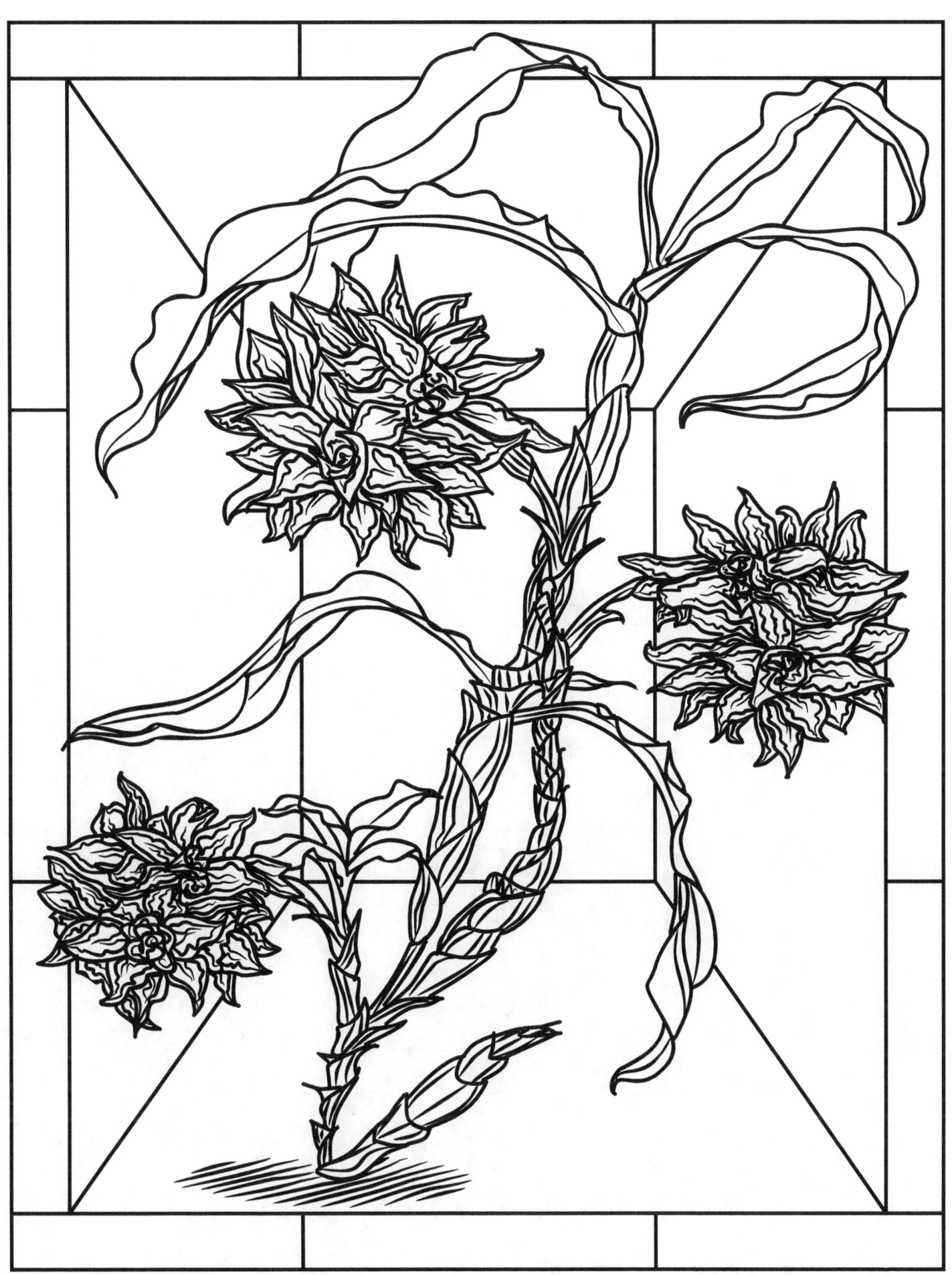